CW00468594

# Human Ocean
## POEMS

*By*
*Sam Bloomfield*

*"Magical poems from a young poet whose
images open you to the fullness of life."*

— Professor Peter Hawkins

# Human Ocean

Copyright: Sam Bloomfield 2015

ISBN: 978-0-9930711-0-2

Front cover design by Ian Rank-Broadley FRBS
Back cover photo by Barbara Manzi-Fe, 2014

*Second Edition*
*First published in the UK by*
Winslade
193 Slad Road
Stroud, GL5 1RG
winmarkgraphics@me.com

*with the kind assistance of*
Chrysalis Poetry
5 Oxford Terrace, Uplands
Stroud, Glos. GL5 1TW

**OTHER TITLES IN THIS SERIES:**
*Falling into Grace*—Angie Spencer
*Venus Reborn*—Kate Firth
*Still Waiting*—Valerie Denton
*Meetings on the Edge*—Chris Vermeijden
*Between Two Worlds*—*a series of sonnets*—Diana Durham (USA)
*Golden Shadow*—Polly Howell
*Out of This World*—Jay Ramsay
*Sirens Singing in the Grey Morning*—Rupert M Loydell
*Home All Along*—Rupert M Loydell
*The Difficult Gate*—Jehanne Mehta
*Mysterium*—Marion Fawlk
*Gita – a dialogue of love and freedom*—Jay Ramsay
*Enlivenment*—Lynne Sedgemore CBE
*Zoetrope*—Geoff Mead

# Human Ocean

## POEMS

*By*
*Sam Bloomfield*

*For Lioba*

The night sky is full of sunflowers
and the ocean is your mirror.

# Foreword

This second edition includes at times substantial and minor revisions. Sometimes this has been to correct typos or take out extraneous words. In other instances performing the poems over the last year to audiences in the UK and India, sharing them with friends, collaborating with other artists, especially with Laurel Pyne, has meant a refining and deepening of my understanding of the themes these poems raise, and the rhythms and cadences they express. This may sound strange, yet layers of meaning are generated beyond the rational or conscious mind, and some of the layers were not open to me at the time of writing them. There are of course intended implicit and at times fairly explicit subtexts and carefully chosen motifs, yet some of the metaphors have a life of their own.

I include three new poems as they express something like a conclusion to the chapter of my life that this book attempts to share. They also point you in the direction of the next book of poetry, which I am in the maelstrom of writing.

*Sam Bloomfield*
*Stroud, November 2015*

# Contents

# Beloved

Come walk with me
Let's dine under the few great trees
Together we'll sing to the skies
And skip off tall grasses
Into the flower fragrant air
With wide, wide smiles.

Beloved
Come take my hand
We'll caress the air around dragonflies
Together melt into the water
With tears brimming in our eyes
Doggy paddling into the ecstasy of being alive.

Beloved
Come dance with me
We're in the greater heart of the mother
Our feet like upward spirals
Have turned the ground
Into a flower fruiting orchard
Where only love is found.

# All the way in

As the crowd sang a gentle song of forgiveness
cars that used to cruise the streets
settled into a vast bank of pebbles.
birds gathered their wings
and span their spinning feet into tarmac
traffic hungry folk, now walking
ground to a halt and started humming
like a swarm of bees
before settling… all the way in.

# Earth-body

**Earth**

What is this body but you? Mother.
We are the earth:
Each of us seed and egg, pollen and fruit,
from your sky-framed store.
Here with my flesh I call you,
and you are feet, hands, face.
What is this body but you? Mother.
Each of us one of your give-aways.
As we choose to love you we root,
as we chose to love the light
we form our stem.
As we release the past with love we flower,
as we love each other without any need other than to love
so do we bear fruit.

**Fire**

Welcome licking tongues of flame,
welcome soft warmth,
welcome raging heat,
devouring senses, projections and selves.
We are all burning, dry wood
in the furnace of the inner sun,
kindling in the beloved's ever-moving hands of light.
Welcome candle to burn in the darkness of my prayer.
Welcome burst of light to pull me upright.
Welcome spirit, enraged with love.

## Air

Each of us is a thin reed standing
at this cosmic season in a storm of breath,
breath on mountain, breath over sea, breath into fire.
Spirit you shout in our ears
then you whisper through the cracks in my heart
of unity
You call me with your ten thousand voices,
in your ten thousand tongues and
breathe me into life, again, again.
What is there but to be breathed
and surrender all our music to you?

## Water

Bearing, crushing force and mass, yet softer than velvet,
softer even than my lover's skin
sweet to taste, to trickle, to wet,
to caress my inside and my outside.
Who are you?
Bearer of rhythm, of tide, of emotion,
of waves of salty tears
and rivers of passion.
Where were you born?
You!
Who are deep cold mirror
and frothing steaming spring.
You!
Who can and will carry everything away.
Sand, stone, rock and bone, and birth all anew.

# Sam

There is a child in the man
longing for soft, milk filled skin
and that is ok.
There is a victim in the man
saying there is something wrong with the child
A hollow voice echoes through him; 'I am not ok.'
There is a distance within he does not know how to bridge
even with a three-year-old's big eyes.
His father was too far from home to touch.
There is his mother's anger dance
that takes him by surprise
there is his very own cutting off where
he goes cold and does not care
to cope without love.

Now, every day I call him back
I stroke his limbs, chest, face and hair
find his heart and plant seeds of love in there
I just ask him to bear to feel
not to blame or run
when the fear comes day or night
when the anger at not having
makes him fight and hurt
so that before his eyes go
hard and cold in victory or defeat
he can hear the voice of love
and soften to the touch.

# In the cave

In the cave
of my loneliness there sits
an old man
an old woman
they are knitting
together
knitting a jumper for me to wear.

# My heart is black with grief

My heart is black with grief
I deserted my tired lover
my behaviour blaming her
mind running from responsibility
body running to whomever

My heart is black, as an eternal cage,
see the crack, in my self-image,
the ridiculous man who refused to see
self-created loneliness stalking him.
Instead I tore myself from love
wielding a knife to the delicate silk of a marriage bed

My heart is turned from the sun
charred and splintered, wholly undone.
This my own creation yet comes
from the childhood of a man
whose father left in fear
whose mother held suffering in judgement.
This comes to a man who burns the house of the beloved
it's timbers high above him.

I do not know how to forgive my betrayal
of a father's promise to his son
but I alone may welcome this shadow
to the place where my heart was
until its work is done
and sit with the absent father, who I now am
through many nights and days
until he can tell of what undid him
and what will make him whole again.

# The night-long

The night-long
melting into the darkness
falling into ecstasy through intimacy.
I look up at the sky and have a vision.
The trees are talking to me.
"Yes." They say.
"Thank you for holding each other through the night
under our outstretched arms.
The others didn't notice our invitation."

# It is the flesh and form of you

It is the flesh and form of you
that makes my heart sing
yet like a sea seeking fish
sings to the ocean
this is how I desire you.

It is the wet embrace of
your lips and tongue
that quickens my pulse
yet like rainfall
hurtles to the ground
this is how I am drawn to you.

It is the bright tree top soul
of your eyes
that reflect my hidden
beauty back to me
yet like sunlight causes
the explosion of spring
this is how I grow when you gaze on me.

And as this earth
is far more than fertile soil
so are you much more
much more than your beauty
as your breath whispers into me
I melt into the bliss of silent being
like a still night sky cloaks the earth.
And when you call my given name
that same self is blown from it's stem
like ripe dandelion seed
in the heat of a late summer storm.

I see into you and you are
full with sky reaching trees,
fast flowing rivers, diamonds
and deep dive pearls.
There, beyond the smooth touch
of your soft skin and
the luminescence of your
long lashed eyes, there
is the eternal perfection
of your untamed
wild and laughing soul.

# Us

her; lithe, long, me; swollen tight like ripe grapes,
skin-tight, clasped by disbelief,
the drum beats, hearts beat, mouths meet

like leopards, untamed we prowl in the shadows,
skirt the civilized flame
like it's a small, failing, flickering fantasy

and then leap, scattering any stuck-ness in the brain,
embers flying, resistance dying,
sparks flying to the four directions

breath to breath, leaping into the canopy of air anchored,
tree bound fertility, breathing her in,
her breathing me in, into shared sanity

writhing, shedding skins, grinding into hips,
face, skin slipping, clambering,
finding strong brown limbs as branches

biting, wrestling, wet lick, claws teasing skin,
scratching to the ground, feline fecund lips,
sweet scented sap, belly cunny bound

panting, lips to lips, buds to buds, tongue to teeth,
climbing down, inside the cambium,
down toward the ground

vine ripened wine spilling on skin,
red tender delicate flesh, sweetly scented,
shame-free liquid running, chasing desire

falling, splashing, purring, licking into wetness found,
then gone, gone, shape shifted, gone
she is a spirit form, flying high

skimming treetops, wings brushing the reaching leaves,
we both escape the orgasm
of capture, release and rest

there is a black-winged rushing, flying to the moon
in a black sky, reeling, spinning, leaving,
wind beating our minds into lucid light

hawk arching, magpie colliding, ravens calling,
soul contact! Feathering in, back in,
seeking safety from crying, cavorting.

Her; eyelids half closed, crimson-stained nipples
softening, seeking solace, from birthing to dreaming,
from male to female thinking.

Me; scrying, softly roaring, hearing soft echoes
of dancing, drumming giving way to a drone,
dying giving way to dreaming.

# I am a bird flying through the night calling to the moon

I found the moon with you last night,
she was waiting for us as our bodies lay
chest to chest, thigh to thigh
she was soaking up
droplets of sweat from our bellies
breathing great sighs of relief.
She doesn't meet enough love-making and
she's fed up with crying over battlefields.
She tells me that romance is underrated.
"As long as you keep the thousand names
of the beloved on your lips."
I have travelled before, made love before,
seen the stars and felt the blue of the cosmos
wash over me.
I can dive into warm water
meditate my way to the sun,
but only you took me to the moon
and bathed me in her light.
She is such a soft mirror, such a delicate soul.
How does she look down at all this and feel it all?

Soft tears fall to my lap as I sit with you both.

# The edges of love are sharp

Rejection rises and cuts at the
skins of old memories
trying to find their secrets
but the incisions only reveal more layers
I am holding a weapon when I need a ladle instead...
After all, the pot is boiling nicely on the stove.
A few drops of salty tears
and old hurts have become a healing stew.

# Hello love's shadow

Welcome.
I invite you to sit at my bed
even as my lover breathes into my ear
presses her whole naked self into me
even as I feel the joy of unity
I see your jealous eyes
am touched by your pale cold hands.
Come to the fire in my heart, warm yourself,
come doubts, come fears, come tears
you are also welcome.
Come uncertainty, come loneliness, come ugliness
this heart is big enough for you all.
Sit and share your stories with me.
As a child I ran from you,
slamming doors, escaping
into rooms lined with painful faces,
but now, but now
You are my way into the light
we stand together,
holding hands, sharing tears, walking into this night
step by step.

# Finding myself alone

A few days of togetherness and I find faults,
like a craftsman looking for scratches
as if you are the inside of my mouth
and my mind is my tongue.

I find the fantasy of you so attractive
that I would rather run
than discover the feeling of being loved,
while it seems so close to being smothered.

The key turns in the lock, front door opens,
warm smells, good smells; sage, flowers
but no one other than me to turn the lights on…

My fingers reach out in the dark.

# There is

There is a small child inside
sometime laughing
sometimes crying
once or twice despairing.

Look after this lover of life.
inner jewel
your hope-filled friend
who waits for you.
Warm to this love
And the hearth in your heart,
will burst into flame.
Sit by the fire of what was lost
and eat toast together with sticky fingers again.

# Storm

Wind moves through trees
Branches sway in chaos
My soiled roots hold firm.

# It is singing

Your heart has it's mouth open
awesome and wide as a whale's.

Will you flood into this catastrophic
cathedral of transformation?

And with a rush of blood
discover you are one.

With all the other big and small fish
in this fish-eating, sacred ocean.

Can you dive the depths
below any shoreline?

Find the deep stillness
in the centre of your heart.

Now. Where never a word is spoken
but sung.

Dare you?

# What is there but this?

What is there but this?

And is this full of joy, of light, of love,

of splendour?

If there is anything, anything

holding you back from laughing and crying at

the ecstasy of creation

quietly tell a friend and make a pact.

Go out together and yell, dance, sing

generally make love with the universe.

Who knows what might happen?

God might be listening, tear off her clothes and join in!


Now, what is this!?

# Don't let that bastard life grind you down

White unopened envelopes on the table
not wiped from the night before
crumbs of old food…
a three quarters empty bottle of wine.
Don't let that bastard life grind you down
bills, bills, bills, yet more bills
and the old people you know are too slow to die
don't let that bastard life grind you down.

You live in a terrace, the next-door neighbours
have terriers and screaming children
bills, bills, bills, and DIY.
Don't let that bastard life grind you down
no-ones really grateful to you
for anything you've done and done well
trees planted late at night
the sacrifices you made
good decisions only you know about
that will never make you famous.
That is you.

Don't let some bastard idea grind you down
life is incredible, wonderful, beautiful
it's Beltane, Oester and Lilith,
snaking to the sky
it's big fluffy white clouds
grimy pubs you can walk past

it's elderly people hobbling along the pavement
still bloody grinning
it's blue skies, even if they are so far away
you cannot touch them
and the sun is still resolutely shining
if not on your face then on someone else's.
So let this awesome mystery of life lift you up, lift you up
until at the end like a flower you burst
and like the wind you are gone.

# Look whichever way

Dust like Victorian London smog
Dogs lying in the way
Brown bony bodies
Worshiping God
God of everything
God of everywhere
God of burning plastic
Of people dying, no! Living
On the street
God of neon Kali statues
Of blind staring eyes
God of begging, of poverty
Of hovering mosquitos
Market sellers and hungry flies
God of black tobacco teeth
And impossibly
Deep, deep eyes and
Improbably white, white joyful smiles
God of urine pooled
Rutted earth bus stations
And restaurants like pavements
Run by 10 year old teenagers
Rolling pots like cauldrons and eyes
That have seen too much
God of flawless skinned children
As bright as flowers
Riding home from school,
As bright as this wide arc of day
Oh God
Of road side spitting, shade sitting

Full-bellied men and
Working women bent double in rice fields
God of anything
God of everything
God of everywhere
God of India.

# Welling up

A teardrop.
All the emotion of war
loss and
the uncontainable
pictures
in this one
syllable of the eye,
so bright.
Indicator
of feeling
that you wipe away
in a moment
or let fall
and fall again.
Like God's people
fallen and imperfect
so someone can claim
you need mending.
From walking on water
to praying for penitence,
when there is nothing, nothing
imperfect
about even this one tiny sea
hanging from eyelashes
curved in divine ratio.

Which crazed rational fool

ever convinced an army
to fight
in this garden of contour,
ridges, rounds, peaches, pears
and thrusting branches
with arms designed
to lift to this heaven
just here
and pluck fruit
and plant trees.
Not tear them up
not rape her furrows.
But given to
sink into handfuls of rich soil
teaming with voices.
Not to make weapons
when fingernails are enough
in their delicate hardness.

Consonants can hurt
when we are connected.
What is this conflict
we sustain with sheer stubbornness.
What is this fallacy we allow
each one of us,
when a human rises with hatred
and walks booted and rough
over this land bright with feeling
delicate as children singing.

# Day by Day

Before I wake
I cup
The sky
The trees
The hills
Into vast hands
That are not mine
Then
With the dawn
Nature expands
And I
Once as
Infinite as night
Awake
An industrious ant
With mortgage
And failing sight

But unconscious sleep awaits..

My
Night by night
Lover
Dark fountain of breath
Healer
Leading me
To remember
Demanding I forget
Turning off the light
So that moth-like
In a moment of
Perfect solitude
I become
A burnt offering
To the collective
Mystery of night.

# When we say

I feel.
We invite the heart
the love, the joy
the passion of human vulnerability
to dance in the space
between us, we suckle into faltering steps
the frail winged bird of compassion.
And when we deeply listen, listen beyond words
lose ourselves in listening
we invite the spirit, the love, the ecstasy
our reverence for all human beings
to transform the most broken life,
the heart tearing open, again and again,
to heal again.
Mine and yours.
And when we consciously speak
with tongues, hands and feet,
the truth,
that we can only ever hurt ourselves.
And drop our masks, shake off the armour
of our self judgments and
ride the dragon of truth naked,
yes naked, even through the clinging mist
of our pretence sodden culture,
then we are alive you and I
then we realise death is coming
closer with each breath
and if not to live now, then when,
then when?

# Woman

Soft in satin fabric
Gently draped in desiring,
Semi-dressed in mandalas
Hair flowing in rivulets
Drawing my gaze and blood,
Brown skin, flushing pink.
Lace and spirals,
Down silver sleeves,
With a twist and a twirl,
Heart persistently beats.
A flash of green eyes
Lined and lashed, dressing, undressing
With the scent of her underneath
Touch of her so close
Nature's animal,
Goddess, almost in heat.

# It's not

It's not
Death.
It's not
Taxes.
It's
Love.

# Delectable

Delectable
lips
are
a way in
to
Love

So is slowly
saying
the
word

delectable.

# Rose

Your petals, so fleshy and scented
made by the body of the great mother
once hidden in the dark clutch of the earth
you quiver releasing more perfume to my touch
become flushed at the tender flicking of my tongue
framed by shades of dark and pink satin.
Human rose.

# In the song of life

Where the butter is kept cool
and toast pops up, hot and steaming
in the everyday where light streams in
through the open door and a gentle breeze
caresses my skin

In the abundance of living
where I share my joys and tragedies
and just open to intimacy with you
this is where I want to be my love

Here in my arms, in your arms
fully free, fully committed
to the song of life in the everyday
spreading strawberry jam on sourdough rye

Swinging children by their hands
and eating wild harvest on long walks
singing my life song to you,
to the green trees, the rippling sea
this my love is where I want to be.

# The Risk

I was lost, I couldn't find myself in the faces I saw.
Look at me, am I broken?
What is this body for?
Can I dance, can you dance?
Why are we sitting, looking, waiting, staying quiet, not
saying, holding in tension,
until …we make ourselves ill?
What are we afraid of?
…Will you judge me, ridicule me, laugh at me?
What if I am myself, if I break free
From mechanical patterns of mediocrity
…What will happen?
Will I cry?
If I take a risk and dance around the kitchen,
Will I laugh?
If I take a colleague by the hand and waltz down the corridor
will we cry out for more?
If I say to life; 'I embrace you!'
And give back fully with every limb.
What if we all let our bodies sing?
Together return the bright world once more.
Together suck the breath of life to our core.

# Eye Gazing

I love you like when I first saw you
And now love you deeper than before
knowing that soon with laughter in my eyes
I'll love you even more

My darling
all this is nature-bound to pass
but in the mean time
lets create it to last

I love it when we are apart
I crave the longing and rejoice in being poor
then I soak the intimacy in when I'm with you
And my heart keeps saying yes to more

My darling
the light has to turn to dark
but in the night let's hold on tight
and remember to let go when it's bright

I'm a fool for the heights,
I'm a poet for the suffering
I sing to love when I'm on my own
and I'll sing to you when you're at home

My darling
all this is nature bound to pass
but we have years of adventure
and learning ahead of us

Sometimes I don't understand you
and I play right out of tune
then at times one of us is down
While the other plays the clown

Oh my darling
hair is blocking the sink
and the dishwasher is on the blink
Life has got so damn busy I cannot think, but

I love you like when I first saw you
and now love you deeper than before
knowing that soon, with tears in my eyes
I'll love you even more

# Letter From An Indian

This is a red rose in the sea
 A red rose coming for you.
The petals are vast, and will
swallow your Western mind like a gnat.
How can you Westerners help but love us?
See how generous we are,
so generous we will sell you everything nearly
my friend, nearly everything.

For Khrisna has your soul too, you know.
You cannot sell a man's soul
You cannot sell a woman's soul.
And our Indian nation silently
prays for the soul of the world.
With fire, with water, with milk, with muscle,
everything the great mother gives us,
because humanity is blind.
This is the time of darkness
This is the time of blindness.

We are all bumping into this world.
Trying to find, to sell and buy
answers to this great mystery.
Buy Yoga and you can yoke the mind
back to the body, back to the body
this is the unifying practice
and takes and rewards great effort
leading to a narrow path made
with the fingers and toes of saints,
prophets, poets and acrobats.

Then there is the wing of the heart
the spirit wing and this
you cannot buy from anyone,
however masterful they appear.
It will only take flight with grace
no effort required, no straining to keep pace.
Spirit is not a being
you can push into alignment
It is a being of itself. It is.
Always the first trigger. It is.
That is why you are still
searching for it with your
western mind. Still searching
for the cause you will not find.

Yet this is fine in it's flatness
just a reflection of human sadness
and the sun gives ceaselessly
to the earth from high above,
and the earth turns it's rays
into plenitude and love.

And here all the while is the rose in the sea
the vast rose, just waiting
for you to open your nostrils
and breathe her in, and come to me
and she will breathe you out
until you have become her scent
and now mystery is all you can perceive.
And you are taken up
A feather of awe on a great wing
The peace, the love, perhaps even
God is breathing you in.

# From La Corbière

Thundering. Crashing.
Drifts of pebbles rolling. You.
Driving a horizontal storm towards the deep red rocks,
you, a pure white foaming mist of salt
gyrating with a flood of golden sand.
I love you. You are so utterly unrelenting.
Your spray glistens on the hard stone
skin worn smooth over millennia.
So soft you slip between my fingers like my lover's hair
yet so crushing that you thunder from miles out
a rocking pulsing torrent of raw power.
I will not stand in your way.

My whole life as fleeting
as the dazzling flecks of golden sun
on your tumultuous surface
but I cannot turn away from you,
towards the repressed 'safety' of land
I have to return again and again
to marvel at your coarse grace
to have visions of licking your brooding whipping tongues.
to be stunned by your throaty, clear, cold, exhilaration.

Like great yelling hoards of warriors
you assault the stiff coast,
throwing yourself over rocks and over rocks again
to scatter and thrash high in the air.
running your dripping tongues
over the jutting stones
over and over.
Agh you beast!
You fervent, unrelenting, devouring beast

so vast I no longer need to look to the sky to feel
utterly small and windswept.
It was an unemotional thought
that my kind could ever think
to conquer you
I should merely grovel before your total supremacy
we should, were we sane,
run like little shadows to the woods and lakes for safety
but we don't.

Who are you Great Mother?
Who sculpts your ever-changing tidal face?
What awesome Blakeian power dare even now contain you
between rock and sand?

But am I left lonely and afraid
on this outcrop of sun-warmed rock
as you thunder towards me? Or
as I gaze at you am I like an animal
surrendering to graceful death?
Yes! Yes! You inflame my deepest passion for annihilation.
Your beating, massing form sucks me into an ecstasy
of shrieking and whooping.
I thirst for life as you confront me
and then I am gone
I am lost in you, in your foam
and then in your green blue opaque reserves of terrible power
I am lost in the miles and miles of peaks and distant shadows
that are your ever changing engulfing skin.

Come on! I roar into your spray
you drown me out completely,

yet we are in unison and
I become your bellowing breathing passion
with my tiny lungs.
Whatever once made you, whatever sustains you;
also loves me
you are brother to my male, mother to my child.
And you are my harrowing lover,
seething at the delicate fragrance
of my most succulent parts.

You are my womb bearer, and my very inner body
you are in me to the middle of my bones
your cresting is like the wave on wave
that floods me during orgasm.
even the salt of my body is your kin
in taste and teeming potency.
I have to get closer
and you assault my skin now, yes!
Soak my remaining clothes in a cold rush of sexual frenzy
as if I were subsumed in you already.

I leap up
and rush to climb the tallest outcrop of rock at your edge,
dripping with your saliva
woken from my fantasy of love making
by your quenching cold touch.
And the setting sun comes amber
from under a great stretch of cloud.
And you froth and charge at me again,
grasping at my toes
yet I cling on to rock
to be next to you but not with you, just yet

daring the darkness as she too grows around us
I am in a fever of natural lust
oh for you to overwhelm me like Whitman!
As the reddening light again bathes the rocks
We are both wet and scattered before you,
you sacred charging beast,
your foam churning and lathering as I cry out.

A mist of your scented spit dances around us.
The sun too has become liquid now,
a glowing ball melting into you,
your horizon framed by perfectly motionless clouds
and then here is my mind again
 my fragile self
poised between an infinity of space
and your laughing, exalting mass.
I write this love poem to you,
you now oil dark and glistening bringer of life.
I am calling to you, mistress of me, of this world.
I pray to you as the tears spill from my eyes.
I know You will take me at my end,
that you have taken me and all of us
again and again, birthed and re-birthed me at death
beyond my human understanding I have risen from you.
The swathe of clouds light up from below,
a bright burning red
…and I slip away into a softly heaving ,
gently breathing, dusk.

# Acknowledgements

Thanks to the dear friends who accompanied me on this journey and helped me find love again when I had become blind to it, especially Nikki, Anna, Amy, Sam and Eliza.

In the same vein thanks to Will Gethin for his searing honesty, for wading into his shadow discoveries, and making me jealous enough to continue writing myself.

Thanks to Ian Rank-Broadley for his unfailing commitment to the muse, for risking everything for the greatness of his art, and for instilling in me a love of this ever changing human form.

Thanks to Greg Tricker for the spirit in his artworks that inspire me to celebrate the sacred in the most simple acts of caring.

Thanks to Rupert Sheldrake for daring to stop dissecting frogs and campaign for scientific integrity and common sense while furthering our understanding of how the world may work through his piercing intelligence.

Thanks to Jay Ramsay for his insistence that we are all brave enough to turn this weary human world back to sacred love. Dear Jay – my deep gratitude for asking me to gather these poems together, embracing my love of the didgeridoo and inviting me to perform with Phoenix over the years.

Thanks to Bruce Winslade for his skills and generosity in preparing this book for publication. It could not have found a more amenable or jocular midwife.

Heart felt thanks to Nick Clements, Fred Hageneder, Gaston St. Pierre, Hans-Konrad-Peyer and Veronique Munoz-Darde for paying me to help them edit, write or translate.

A father's thanks to Dion, Olivia, Gabriel and Anouk for being so patient while I needed to daydream, and teaching me about the path of heart over and over again. Without all of you life would be so dull.

Thanks to Ella for inspiring me with her beautiful poems and ridiculous sense of humour.

Thanks to Gaston St Pierre again for being my mentor, friend and confidant. I am very grateful to the many participants at Metamorphic Technique workshops I taught over the years. You brought so much creativity and insight to me. Especially thanks to Jo Bowers for waiting so patiently at La Corbière, and Gaston for still being.

Finally, deepest thanks to Barbara, Roger, David and Malmfrid. The four of you provided the finest ingredients. I had to mix them up and do the baking myself. It's been messy, but a lot of fun.

*"These poignant and sensitive poems about love and loss reveal a great deal about the poet himself. Always ready to share emotionally, Sam embraces humanity with words of great subtlety and feeling."*
— Ian Rank Broadley FRBS

*"Sam Bloomfield's poems are part of Nature, and exude all his wonderful characteristics of honesty, passion, playfulness, sensitivity and beauty alongside an incisive awareness of the things that matter most for us now. He's an 'artist healer', one of a new tribe with ancient roots. He also has a distinctive lyric gift, like the true poet he also is read on/in bed, aloud...*
— Jay Ramsay

*"For me Sam's words take the form of a terrier dog who has the satisfaction of getting his teeth firmly gripped onto a favourite toy. He firmly shakes and pulls, and by doing so concepts, ideas, images and fragments tumble out and are revealed.*
— Professor Nick Clements

*"Echoes of Rumi from a deep lover of life and wild explorer of love and soul – these beautiful poems by Sam burn bright with passion and are imbued with the visceral power of nature and truth."*
— Will Gethin, Founder of Conscious Frontiers

**Sam Bloomfield**
started writing
poetry at 15 as
a response to
unrequited love,
while at Wynstones
Steiner School.
He is a body
reflexologist, healer,
didgeridoo player,
teacher, facilitator,
performer, support
worker, author,
writer of long lists
and trainee Dance
and Movement Psychotherapist working in Bristol.

As a very young man he worked as a labourer and in demolition and as a tree surgeon. He went to UCL and was awarded a first class double honours degree in political philosophy and german literature. Sam went from modelling for life size bronzes in Ian Rank Broadley's studio, to collaborating as a body print artist. Following a creative impulse he also acted in a Commedia dell'Arte show at the National Theatre. He was lucky enough to meet Rupert Sheldrake and work as a researcher for him, before then going into healing full time for seven years. He became a manager and emotional literacy trainer for Ruskin Mill Trust for another seven years. Put all of that together with being twice divorced and no wonder he is a poet.

Contact Sam and stay in touch with his work through *www.sambloomfield.org* or *www.sambloomfield.org.uk*